LEVEL HEADERS

Stretch your CONFIDENCE!

written by
Beth Cox

in collaboration with
Power Thoughts founder
Natalie Costa

illustrated by
Vicky Barker

www.bsmall.co.uk

Published by b small publishing ltd. www.bsmall.co.uk © b small publishing ltd. 2019 • 1 2 3 4 5 • ISBN 978-1-911509-96-7
Production: Madeleine Ehm   Publisher: Sam Hutchinson   Editorial: Sam Hutchinson   Design and Art direction: Vicky Barker   Printed in China by WKT Co. Ltd.
All rights reserved. No reproduction, copy or transmission of this publication may be made without written permission. No part of this publication may be reproduced, stored in a retrieval system or transmitted in any form or by any means, electronic, mechanical, photocopying, recording or otherwise, without the prior permission of the publisher.
British Library Cataloguing-in-Publication Data. A catalogue record for this book is available from the British Library.

How this book works

This book is full of activities to help you stretch your confidence and overcome nerves. The activities all build on each other so are designed for you to work through in order, but you can skip some and go back if you want, or dip in and out if you'd rather - there are no rules.

Use the icons to find top tips, useful information, suggestions for taking it further, and details of additional resources.

Useful info/fact

Take it further

Top tip

Make your own

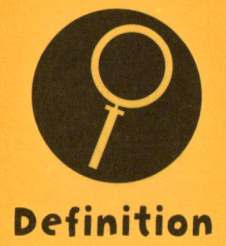
Definition

What is confidence?

Imagine a muscle in your body. You can't really see it but the more you exercise and stretch the stronger it gets. Confidence is also like a muscle. It gets stronger the more you use it. Do you remember the first time you tried to ride a bike? You probably felt a bit scared at first but with practice you became a confident cyclist. What is really important is that you had the courage to try in the first place and the strength to have another go if you fell off.

How confident you feel can depend on the situation. Maybe you feel really confident about schoolwork, but not so confident about making new friends and fitting in. Or it could be the other way round. How confident you feel changes all the time and your confidence changes as you grow up and get older. The more experiences you have, the more chances you have to stretch your confidence muscle.

Contents

4-5	Your strengths	20-21	Learning pods
6-7	The 'In' crowd	22-23	Grow your brain
8-9	Friendship wobbles	24-25	Champions of change
10-11	Courageous you	26-27	Stepping stones
12-13	Brave bodies	28-29	What's the problem?
14-15	Picture this	30-31	Give it a go!
16-17	Distract yourself	32	Never give up!
18-19	Make fear your friend		

Your strengths

What are you good at? It can be easy to focus on the things you find tricky. Being aware of the things that you want to improve is good, but let's start by looking at what you CAN do.

"The one thing that you have that nobody else has is you. Your voice, your mind, your story, your vision."
- Neil Gaiman

"Real confidence comes from knowing and accepting yourself – your strengths and your limitations."
- Judith M. Bardwick

I can ride a bike.

I can follow instructions.

I can make my friends laugh.

I can

I can... _

I can... _

I can... _

I can... _

I can... _

I can... _

Everyone has different strengths. What are yours?

Draw or stick in a picture of you doing something you really enjoy. In the frame write all the strengths and skills, big and small, you use to do that thing.

If you find it hard to write about what you can do, try doing this activity for a friend first. Sometimes it can be easier to see the strengths of your friends first.

The 'In' crowd

There will be times when you feel like you just don't fit in with everybody else. Feeling like this can make you start acting, dressing or speaking differently. But, because you are not being yourself, you still feel like you don't fit in. **Absolutely everybody feels like this at some point.**

Often a social group forms because of just one thing people have in common. Maybe it's liking tennis or even just wearing the same style of coat! But groups based on just one thing don't tell us everything about the people in them. If you choose a different thing to base the group on, the people in it would be completely different. The more you find out about people, the more ways of grouping them you will find. So you will always fit in somewhere, or with someone — if you're not similar to someone in one way, maybe you're similar to them in another way?

 **Finding something you have in common is a great way to make friends. It might be music, books, food, sports... but remember, we are all different and like different things, so you won't have something in common with everyone.**

"Friendship is born in that moment when one person says to another: 'What, you too? I thought I was the only one.'"
- C S Lewis

Ways of grouping people

- Eye colour
- Clothing
- Style
- Interests
- Hair colour
- Age
- Hobbies

Friendship wobbles

We all fall out with our friends from time to time and it can feel horrible. But it's completely normal to disagree with people, even if you like them a lot. The best way to fix a friendship wobble is to talk about it. Rather than just focusing on what someone did, talk about how it made you feel. You could say something like, 'When you pushed in front of me it made me feel like I wasn't important.' Talking about your feelings rather than actions can help to keep things calm.

If you're in a bad mood, you might take your feelings out on others and say something unkind. Or if someone upsets you, your feelings could take over so you say something you don't really mean. Before you speak or act, take a deep breath and ask yourself:

- Is it kind?
- Is it helpful?
- Is it true?

"Say what you mean, but don't say it mean."
- Andrew Wachter

Rewrite these statements, and add some of your own, focusing on how something made you feel rather than what someone else did.

Statement	Say it better
You ignored me.	When you didn't speak to me at lunchtime it made me think you didn't like me.
You took something without asking.	
You told someone my secret.	
You didn't share with me.	

Try using some of your 'say it better' sentences in real life.

Courageous you

Thinking back to situations when you felt confident can help give you courage at other times. For example, if you approach a group of friends with something exciting to share, you probably have a smile on your face, are standing up straight and might be almost bouncing as you walk. Your friends will pick up on this energy and be interested in what you have to say before you've even opened your mouth.

Use that feeling of excitement again in a situation when you know you will feel nervous. You can start to change how you feel and give positive energy to others.

Courage: The ability to do something that frightens one; bravery.

"Courage is resistance to fear, mastery of fear - not absence of fear." - Mark Twain

Draw a picture, stick in a photo or write about a situation when you felt confident.

What were you thinking?

How did it feel in your body?

What were you doing?

Write an action plan for how you can give yourself courage when you don't feel confident.

-
-
-
-
-

Brave bodies

Bodies often give a message about confidence. When you don't feel confident you might keep your body very closed by hunching over, slouching and looking down. But when you do feel confident you probably stand or sit straight, make eye contact and keep your body very open with your arms wide and shoulders back. The way you hold your body gives a message to others. This is called 'body language.'

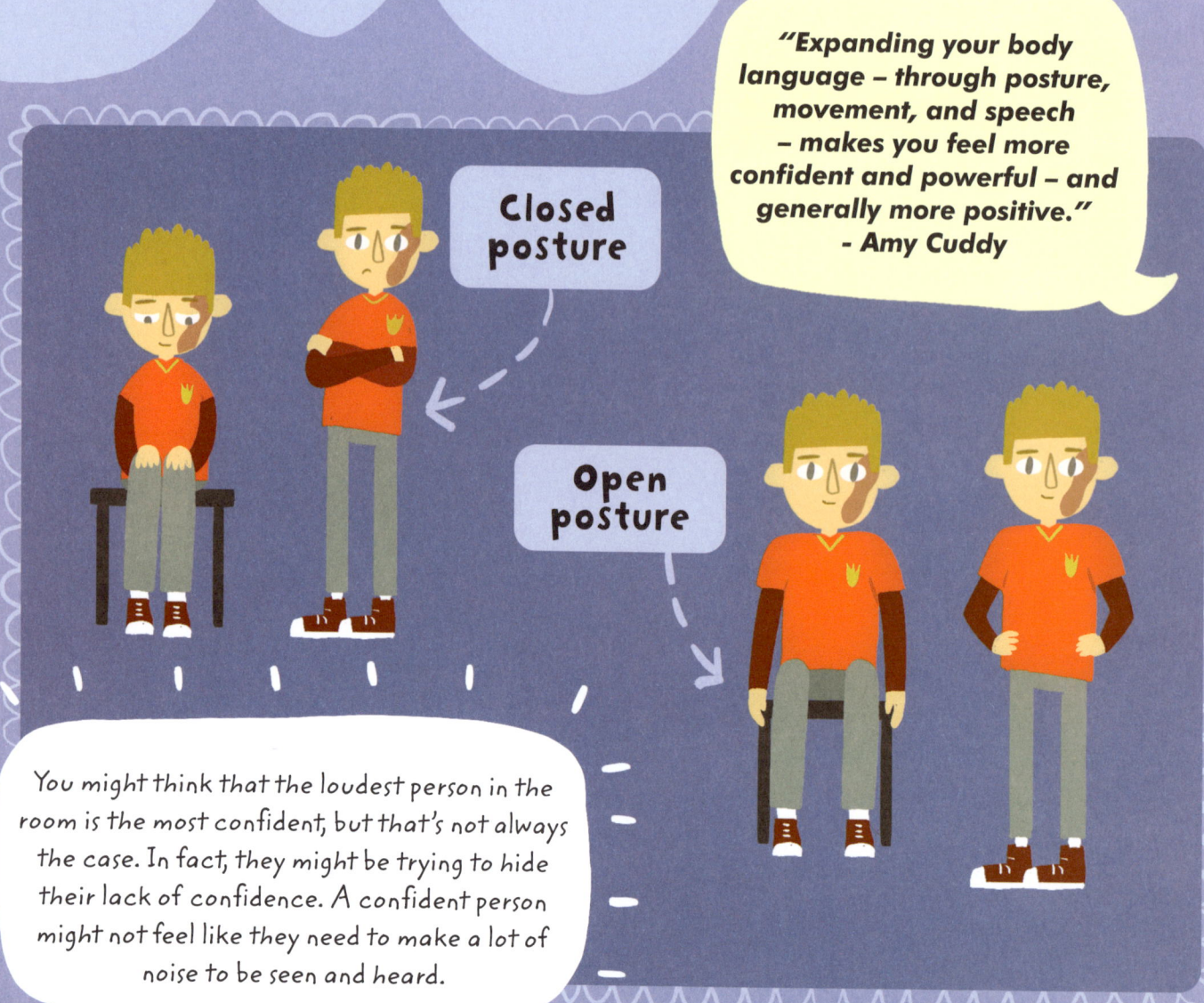

"Expanding your body language – through posture, movement, and speech – makes you feel more confident and powerful – and generally more positive."
- Amy Cuddy

Closed posture

Open posture

You might think that the loudest person in the room is the most confident, but that's not always the case. In fact, they might be trying to hide their lack of confidence. A confident person might not feel like they need to make a lot of noise to be seen and heard.

Picture this

Your imagination is a powerful thing. If you keep telling yourself you won't be able to do something, such as remembering all the spellings for your test, you will worry even more and make it more likely to come true. Luckily, it works the other way. If you can imagine yourself succeeding at something, you will feel more confident about it and that means you are more likely to actually do well.

Imagination and action use the same pathways in the brain. Imagining something is as good as doing it.

"If you can dream it, you can do it."
- Walt Disney

Think about an event that is coming up. Maybe you've got a test, a sporting competition, or an assembly to take part in. Imagine it going well. Write down a detailed description of what happens or draw a detailed picture.

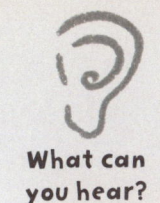

What can you hear?

What can you see?

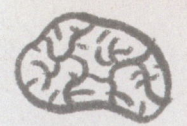

How do you feel inside?

What can you smell?

Make another picture or description to stick up somewhere you can see it regularly.

Play your scene regularly in your head when you are brushing your teeth, on the bus, before going to sleep or at any time.

15

Distract yourself

If you feel nervous about something it can take over and be the only thing you focus on. Finding something to do to distract yourself can be really helpful. You may even forget about your nerves.

Count all the people wearing glasses.

Find all the things that are red.

Count all the flowers, windows and birds you can see.

Find five things you can see, four you can touch, three you can hear.

Reading a story or poem before you do something daunting can also help distract you.

Write an action plan for how you can distract yourself when you are feeling nervous.

- - - - - - -

 Think back to a time something went well. How did it feel in your body? See 'Courageous you' on pages 10 and 11 for more ideas.

Make fear your friend

Fear exists for a reason. It's there to keep you safe. But things that are not dangerous can scare you and that is when fear stops you doing stuff you might enjoy. If you can accept that something is scary and do it anyway, you can take back control and stretch your confidence muscle.

Think about something that you were scared of doing in the past. How did you feel afterwards? Even if things did not happen exactly as you had hoped, you still took the first step.

"Do one thing every day that scares you."
- Mary Schmich

I'm going to ask for help.

I'm going to try a new food.

I'm going to play with someone new.

Challenge yourself to do one thing every day that worries or scares you. Write what you did in the boxes.

MONDAY	TUESDAY	WEDNESDAY	THURSDAY	FRIDAY	SATURDAY	SUNDAY

> Think about something that is hard or challenging and that you need to do or would like to do. It could be big or small. What is it?

What if it all works out?

What could go well?

What makes it worth it?

What happened?

> Take a deep breath and do the thing that scares you.

Think about how you can help a friend who is scared of doing something. You can give yourself the same advice when you have a confidence wobble.

If you want to practise before you actually do it for real, make it fun by role-playing with a friend first.

19

Learning pods

The word 'mistake' is a funny one. It sounds so negative and because of that mistakes feel like a bad thing. But mistakes are actually good. In fact, they help you learn. Learning pods would be a much better name for mistakes, as that is what they actually are. By giving them this more positive label you might feel more positively about them.

Mistakes cause your brain cells to spark and make your brain grow because your brain keeps trying new things until you figure it out.

"Mistakes aren't the opposite of success, they are part of it."
- Arianna Huffington

Grow your brain

When something is hard it can feel impossible. But nothing is fixed forever. You are learning all the time and the more effort you put in, the stronger your brain becomes. Finding something difficult means that you have the opportunity to learn more. This is called 'growth mindset'.

Fixed messages

- I can't.
- It's too hard.
- I got it wrong.
- I give up.
- I made a mistake.
- It's taking too long.
- I'm rubbish at this.
- Everyone else is better than me.

Match the negative (fixed) message to the positive (growth) message.

"All things are difficult before they are easy."
- Thomas Fuller

Growth messages

How can I try this differently?

I wonder how I can do this.

It takes time to learn new things.

If they can manage it so can I.

I can't yet.

With practice I can improve.

This will get better if I keep trying.

What can I learn from my mistake?

Think about the things you tell yourself. Can you change them into growth messages instead?

Champions of change

Change can feel scary and uncertain. It can also feel exciting, fun and new. But most of the time it is a mix of all these things. Whatever it makes you feel, change can help you learn new things, build on your strengths and make you stronger.

In nature, day changes to night and the weather and the seasons change. And in technology, changes happen all the time and really quickly. Hard as it might be to imagine, the internet hasn't always existed!

"If nothing ever changed there'd be no butterflies" - Unknown

Think back to a time when you had to make a change. It might have been starting a new school or class, moving house, making new friends or going to a new club.

What positive things came from the change?

How did you feel?

What did you learn about yourself and others?

How did it make you stronger?

What advice would you give to someone else who is about to make this change?

Stepping stones

Sometimes it is hard to know what you want and even harder to know how to get there. Even if you know what you want to achieve, it can seem too big or too far away. Think of it like crossing a river. If you try to jump to the other side of a big river, you are probably going to fall in. What you need are stepping stones. Take things one step at a time and you will reach your goal.

If your goal is to play your favourite song perfectly on the guitar, the idea that you will make mistakes can put you off. So you never try.

1 Get hold of a guitar

2 Teach yourself one chord

Once you've done that, you can focus on the next steps.

3 Teach yourself the rest of the basic chords

4 Practise each chord

5 Practise switching between chords

6 Teach yourself to play "Twinkle, Twinkle, Little Star".

Now keep going until you can play your favourite song.

"The journey of a thousand miles begins with one step."
– Lao Tzu

What's the problem?

Problems turn up all the time. Often they seem huge, overwhelming and scary... especially if you have no idea how you can solve them. Of course you can ask for help, but most of the time you just need to take a step back to see things clearly.

What's the problem?

Say what the problem is out loud.

Think of at least five possible ways to deal with the problem. Be creative! There are no right or wrong answers.

Brainstorm solutions

Think about the advantages and disadvantages of each solution and pick one to test out.

Choose and do

"Creativity can solve almost any problem." - George Lois

Review

What happened? Think about whether this solution worked and what you might try next time.

Make your own problem-solving template using spare sheets of paper.

Build a tower using just marshmallows and raw spaghetti. How tall can you make it?

Build a bridge using just newspaper and tape. Can it hold a toy car?

Write a riddle to describe your favourite animal without saying what it is. Your riddle should give the reader clues.

Here's an example of a riddle to help you get started:

I'm quite small and furry. I love chasing mice! You can stroke me if you want to. I like to go outside and explore.

Answer : Cat!

29

Give it a go!

When you try something new, thinking about what went well and what did not go well helps you stretch your confidence muscle.

A good place to do this is in the kitchen. Think about foods that should taste horrible together, but actually taste delicious, such as maple syrup and bacon or peanut butter and jam. Someone had to experiment to find out that those combinations work.

"All life is an experiment. The more experiments you make, the better."
- Ralph Waldo Emerson

Salads are a good way to experiment with flavours and textures. Make your own salad. Be inventive and creative with it.

Possible salad ingredients

Nuts and seeds, Kiwi, Orange, Cheese, Watermelon, Lettuce, Olives, Pasta, Tomato, Beans, Carrot, Beetroot, Rice, Couscous, Courgette, Strawberry, Mango, Peppers, Potato

Draw what your creation looked like here.

What did you put in?

What did you do?

What would you change next time?

What did you learn?

How did it taste?

31

Never give up!

It took J.K. Rowling seven years to write the first 'Harry Potter' story. When the book was finished, all the major publishing houses rejected it.

After failing to qualify for the 1968 US Olympic figure-skating team, Vera Wang worked for 'Vogue' magazine as an editor. These are two amazing achievements but Vera kept working hard and trying new things. Now she is one of the most successful wedding dress designers in the world.

The Wright Brothers, Orville and Wilbur, spent years designing, building and testing gliders. After many failed attempts, they became the first people to build an aeroplane that could fly successfully.

Madonna moved to New York with the dream of becoming a professional dancer but found it hard to get regular work. Even as a singer she faced a huge amount of rejection before she finally got a record deal.

Jennifer Hudson went out in 7th place on season 9 of 'American Idol' but has since sold millions of albums and won an award for acting.

Thomas Edison's most famous invention is the light bulb but it took him 10,000 tries before he came up with something that worked.

"I have not failed 10,000 times. I have not failed once. I have succeeded in proving that those 10,000 ways will not work. When I have eliminated the ways that will not work, I will find the way that will work."
- Thomas Edison